Dedicated

This little story is put to the memory of "Dixie and Joe Chapman" who touched the lives of so many.

"Mama Dixie" taught us you can be whatever you want. . . . .just dream and make it happen.

Thank you Mama Dixie and Papa Joe for always encouraging me to believe in myself.

A DOG NAMED TRIXIE

T

Caring for animals can be fun, and give you a new friend. This is a true story of <u>A Dog Named Trixie</u> and her master named Papa Joe. As we get older in life we realize things must change and all good things must end.

Mama Dixie and Papa Joe from the moment we met seemed like family. Mama Dixie was my Business Office Education teacher at the Bibb County Area Vocational School. Papa Joe was the director. Time has a way of passing by because that was 28 years ago.They really loved caring for the students, and after graduation I remained in contact with them.

Tragedy struck this family many times but they always had a positive attitude. Their daughter Donna, died with a brain tumor several years ago and she had a son named Joey who is a pastor and has a precious wife named Heather and three adorable girls. They are in Russia doing missionary work where God has called them to be.

Their other daughter Linda, who married Pete, had a son named Zeeke and a daughter named Megan. Zeeke died from a fire cracker accident in 1988. Through it all the Chapman's kept a positive attitude. Later in life, Megan married a great guy named Aaron and they have two lovely boys full of life.

Papa Joe was a farmer and the greatest farmer on earth.He delivered many vegetables in his lifetime.

As years went by, Mama Dixie and Papa Joe grew old together and were married for almost 66 years. Their favorite song was "I'll Love You Forever and Ever Amen!"

When Mama Dixie passed away about three years ago. Papa Joe was so distraught and lost without her. Well, a dear friend of mine named Judy thought because Papa Joe was lonely she would give him a couple of dogs. Now, these had to be at the time,the ugliest dogs in the world. These puppies were brother and sister. Well, they needed names because Papa Joe's wife was named Dixie. He said,"well I will just name her Trixie and I will name the other one Pete". Pete was easy for him to remember since this was his son-in-laws name. They made the best 'ol squirrel dogs in the world. The only problem was these dogs were not people friendly. They ended up being unfriendly to everyone except their master and chewed up hose pipes, sun hats, shoes, gloves, even shrubs; if you could name it they would chew it. Some of these items happened to be very useful items to their master but he would just laugh and go buy more supplies for Pete and Trixie to chew on.

Trixie loved riding the golf cart and loved to help gather vegetables. Pete on the other hand would rather be chasing squirrels. Pete never did like riding in the golf cart because his master was a wild driver but Trixie said, "If it rolls I am on it".Trixie was thinking "I love riding so much and since they won't allow me in Six Flags the wilder the ride the more fun I can have".The dogs grew up so fast it was hard to imagine them ever being puppies except for they still enjoyed chewing things. Pete finally taught Trixie to squirrel hunt but should the golf cart crank up, Trixie would forget about hunting. Trixie always had the most beautiful smile about her when riding the golf cart. Trixie especially loved for Papa Joe to sing "You Are My Sunshine".

It was a warm summer day and it was time to gather vegetables. Trixie and Pete enjoyed a great breakfast together along with Papa Joe. Pete told Trixie he was going squirrel hunting and Trixie said, "Well I am going golf cart riding". As dawn set in Pete was not home yet from his journey. Trixie knew in her heart something bad had gone wrong so off to look for Pete Papa Joe and Trixie went. It was a sad day for because they found Pete along side the road without any vital signs and bruised up. Trixie was not sure she could go on without Pete but decided Pete got killed doing what he enjoyed best in life and you guessed it squirrel hunting. Papa Joe and Trixie loaded up Pete and wrapped him in a soft blanket and buried him beneath his favorite squirrel tree in the backyard.

It was lonely for several days as Trixie would lie underneath that old tree and did not even want to ride the golf cart. However, as days passed by she made friends with Larry's dog Buddy and they became best of friends. When Buddy was not over eating with Trixie, Trixie was over eating with Buddy. Trixie still did not like people. She enjoyed playing "catch me if you can" and she was always the winner of that game.

Papa Joe was growing feeble, Trixie could tell but then again Papa Joe was just 88 years old. Trixie loved him more each day. Little did they both know tragedy was about to strike again. It was on a cool morning September 27th, 2011. It was a normal day just like any other day. Kim the house keeper arrived about 7:30 am. Kim smelled smoke as she entered the house she had to tell Papa Joe to get out quickly. There was not time to think or get anything. Of course Papa Joe was some what stubborn and thought maybe a fire extinguisher would do the job but Kim had to insist on him getting out. They both made it out fine and watched the house and Toyota 4Runner burn to the ground. Poor Trixie had taken to the woods and watched with grief as some of her squirrel trees were burning down and she was so uncertain of what was about to happen. Just in moments, it was nothing but ashes. Papa Joe only got out with the clothes on his back and not even a pair of shoes. Trixie knew the days ahead would be life changing. As Trixie watched Papa Joe leave with his sweet daughter, Linda, Trixie could not imagine where she would end up. Because of my concern for Trixie I took it upon myself to go by every day to feed Trixie and make sure she had fresh water. Several of the community pitched in as well Bobby and Faye, Joe and Cindy, Larry and Rita, Judy and Bill, William, Little Bobby, Doris,

Kim, and the list goes on. Trixie loved all the food but not any of the humans. Papa Joe was stuck at the Winwood Inn. But not for long and in about four weeks a trailer was put up where the house spot was and once again Trixie and Papa Joe began life together again. Trixie sure had missed those golf cart rides.

By the summer of 2012 Papa Joe was really beginning to slow down. Trixie noticed he did not come out as often but sure was happy when he did. It was that summer that his daughter hired more help which included Kim, Doris, and Wyteria. I myself, was available to do whatever. My main concern was to make sure Trixie had food.Trixie just never did warm up to any of us. Perhaps Doris more than any of the rest of us.

The summer of 2013 Papa Joe had a great garden and started inviting friends to his 91st birthday party in Amory, MS where he had built what he called the Red Barn for his family to meet.Trixie was upset because she was not invited. I would say that 2013 was the best garden Papa Joe ever had. He was the best in the world at raising tomatoes. Even when the Farmers Market did not have tomatoes, he did.We even had fresh garden tomatoes the big day of his 91st birthday party in August. He loved telling people about his garden.However, more than anything, Papa Joe loved sharing his garden. By now Papa Joe was unable to deliver the vegetables but he could ride that golf cart and fill it up. Papa Joe would go inside and start calling friends and by the end of the day, the cart would be empty. Trixie was glad because she had a place to ride come morning.

By Christmas time Papa Joe had thoughts of moving to his daughter's house in Jackson, MS but realized he could not take Trixie and figured him and Pete, the son-in-law just would not get along especially living under the same roof. I think it must have been because they both were too stubborn to admit they both had a streak of stubbornness.

Papa Joe continued to decline. In February his daughter had taken him to the Red Barn. They had a great time except for Papa Joe fell face first on the concrete. Well, because he was so stubborn he told Linda to just wipe the blood off and he would be fine. So off to home they returned which was only about a three hour ride.As they arrived at home his face began swelling. I called Linda and she said daddy needs to go to ER but won't go. I dropped by later that afternoon and getting him to go was like trying to make a mule drink water. Off we went to Bibb ER and he told them they could treat him but he did not want stitches. Most likely he needed stitches but they used a type of glue that worked well.

After a few weeks of healing he looked normal again.Home Health Care started coming by and things seemed to be going as well as they could for someone 91. He was beginning to get garden fever and so was Trixie because that meant going riding on the golf cart. Because Papa Joe was limited, help for the2014 garden had already been put in place.

Papa Joe was tired and by the time March got here he had just about decided I won't even plant a garden. But he ordered some seed just in case. Although, each day he seemed to be slowing down. Trixie sure was glad it was getting close to planting time because it had been a long winter without very many rides.

It was a beautiful warm March day in fact it was March 10th, 2014. It had been a normal morning for Papa Joe and Trixie. The usual sit on the porch, drink coffee, pet Trixie and read the paper. I guess around 1:00 pm his friend Joe stopped by for a long visit. At last the seeds Papa Joe had been waiting for arrived in the mail. By now it was about 2:15 pm in the afternoon and Joe left and told Papa Joe it was a little early to start planting a garden. However he was so excited he decided to go outside and crank the tractor. Trixie was excited as she jumped on the golf cart and little did she know tragedy was about to strike again and this would be her last ride on the golf cart. Papa Joe backed the golf cart up to his shed and Trixie jumped off. Papa Joe was very unstable on his feet and stubborn. He decided he was going to burn some brush before starting the tractor and like most fires it got out of hand. As he was trying hard to keep the fire under control he fell into the fire on his back. The neighbor heard a loud boom and rushed over to find Papa Joe rolling in the fire. She managed to get him out of the fire with assistance of friends. She was truly a hero and saved his life. Trixie was scared and ran to the woods unsure of what had just happened. The shed and her golf cart were destroyed in the fire. The ambulance arrived and Papa Joe according to all those around, said he was in good spirits but he was suffering from some bad burns. Off to Druid City Hospital they rushed him.

I was in Tuscaloosa when I received the call and immediately rushed over to the hospital and called his daughter and she was headed to the hospital from Jackson, MS I was rudely greeted by the guard who acted like Barney Fife and told me I was not allowed to see him and that he was being transported to UAB.My reply was,"Well,he has not left yet". I demanded I see him and he rudely took me back.Papa Joe was smiling as usual and I said,"How do you feel?"He said,"Terrible".As they loaded him in the ambulance, he was still holding it together.He was surrounded by his friends, William and Little Bobby. He arrived at UAB and it was maybe worse than any of us thought.

His daughter arrived and was told at 91 this was going require many weeks in the hospital as well as a long journey to recovery. Tuesday he was still adjusting to what had happened and by Tuesday night his kidneys started failing. He had fought a good fight and by Wednesday morning he was getting very restless. God saw fit to take him home to be with his wife whom we called "Mama Dixie" about 4:30 am.It was truly a shock to our community and hard to believe we had lost him. He had a very nice funeral service and was laid to rest on March 17th 2014, along side his lovely wife in Jackson, MS.

It was hard to think about Trixie but I did go by and feed her each day. Pastor Greg's daughter

Emma said she would take her because she did not have a home but Trixie could not be caught.

As was stated in the author section, I am a real estate agent. When listing a home for sale, people want the house, not a dog or cat. I was beginning to think the sales contract was going to read Trixie remains with the property because you could not catch this dog. Everyone who seemed interested in the property did not want Trixie and I would say this property is being sold "as is" and these potential buyers never called back. You can't blame anyone for not wanting an unfriendly dog. I had spoken with Judy, who had Trixie's brother Snoopy, and she said she could live with them because she had a fenced in yard. That is if we could catch her.

Finally at last my hero Joe, on March 26th comes to my rescue and lasso's Trixie with a blue rope. I was at work when I received this very important phone call, Joe said, "I got Trixie". I said I am on my way because I really thought Joe was kidding. I raced over to Trixie's house and realized I not only had gone through a stop sign but a traffic light as well. We have nice police officers in our town so I knew they would understand. I arrived and Joe did have Trixie feeding her a can of food. It was a real funny sight because while I was trying to put Trixie in the truck the rope got wrapped around the back tire on the truck and since the lasso was not real tight, Trixie almost escaped. We could hear Papa Joe saying "don't hurt my dog son". Luckily we delivered this independent dog to Judy.

But it only took a few days for Trixie to become a house pet. Bill, Judy's husband bought Trixie a pink collar and a pink leash. She is styling walking around the neighborhood singing Amazing Grace how sweet the sound I once was homeless but I have been found I was wild but now I am tame thank God I have a home. Trixie does not like her doghouse and besides she chews everything up. Trixie got really brave one night and found Judy and Bill's bedroom and slept on the pillow with Judy. Trixie got her first dog house with her name on it and a name tag. Trixie rules the house now and her brother, Snoopy, is happy to have someone to play with.

On May 12th, 2014 the place where Trixie grew up was sold and closed. I went to see her and took her a bag of cheeseburgers and chicken nuggets. Trixie was well behaved, happy, pretty, and even loving. Trixie was happy to see me and she really had put on the weight. Judy and Bill had even taken her to the vet and she had been groomed for the first time In her life. Trixie's favorite walk- the woods, nickname - Trix, likes stealing Snoopy's food, and loves napping on the couch. I guess you could say as far as Mr. Chapman's death, today was final as I said in the beginning, "all things must end and what a happy ending for a dog named Trixie".

In closing Papa Joe's cousin Jean, comes to mind. Jean must have 15 cats that she loves and adores. Jean asked me not long ago if I would take care of her cats if she died because she knew her husband Jack would not take care of them. A few days ago she told me there was a person living in her attic and the next day she noticed a cat walking on her roof. Who knows it could have been a squirrel but thank goodness she does not have anyone living in the attic.

Any profits made from this story will go to help other animals find a good home just like A Dog Named Trixie.

Meet The Author:

Thank you for choosing this true story about **A Dog Named Trixie.** My name is Angela Stewart and I am from Centreville, AL I have lived in Centreville all of my life and this is the first story I have published. Many of you who know me, know that cats are the center of my life. I was not a dog person until I met Trixie and she captured my heart.

I graduated from the University of Alabama with a BS degree in HES. I have been a REALTOR since 1990 and have helped many animals find a home during my career. Helping animals like Trixie has always been a top priority. My goal is that this story will help many animals like Trixie find a home.

Please feel free to email me at
AngelaFStewart@aol.com

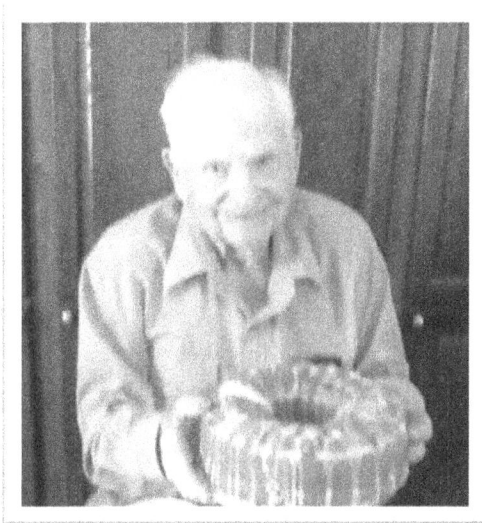

PAPA JOE ON HIS 91ST BIRTHDAY

TRIXIE POSING WITH HER BROTHER SNOOPY

THE END!

www.ingramcontent.com/pod-product-compliance
Lightning Source LLC
Chambersburg PA
CBHW030013040426
42337CB00012BA/761